Rites of Ancient Ripening

Meridel LeSueur

Rites of Ancient Ripening

Mary Ellen Shaw, Guest Editor
Clint Stockwell, Cover Design

*For all the daughters of Changing Woman
—Rachel, Deborah, Madonna, Ellen Moves
Camp, Faith Traversie, Elizabeth, Rosemary,
Devorah, Arlene, Judith and Jocelyn, Robin,
Beth Dora, Rebecca and Meridel Rose, Irene,
Betts, Paula, Linda, Anna, Lasha, Katherine,
Molly, Kimberly, and Dana Jo, and all the
women in Bedlam and in hell and the new
seraphic women, those being born and not
yet born—for all the women of the dark
earth rising into light and freedom.*

"Rites of Ancient Ripening" appeared in
Corn Village, Statton Lee, 1970.
"Shelter Him in Milk and Meadow" appeared
in *Prairie Schooner,* Winter 1969-70.

Pen and ink portrait of the author (back
cover) based on photo composition by
Winston LeSueur.

1st, 2nd, 3rd printings by Vanilla Press
4th printing.
Published by Meridel LeSueur
and David Tilsen.

Printed in the United States of America

IBSN 0-9611098-0-7
(previously ISBN 0-917266-11-0)

INTRODUCTION (or Editor's Aside)

Working with these poems has been like opening a door to an old, well-beloved house; it feels so familiar and "of-course" that it's hard for me to remember that this is the first time I've seen these connections made in poetry — the fecundity of the earth; the spirit in its aspect of the Receptive, of the Feminine; the world-wide, centuries-long sisterhood of nurturance and growth — all so needed now, as the powers of domination and control squeeze this poor planet until it cracks.

It's exciting to be in America right now, where the forgotten comfort of tribal (matriarchal) community still breathes in the wide land and emerges in new dreams of populist power, of organizing cooperatives for our needs (especially for food, medicine, childcare, and other life necessities — social inventions of the first Mother Organizers of infant humanity).

So what this might mean will be a new look at Woman Power — maybe a look backward and inward to help us rediscover something we have been uncomfortable owning. We need to learn that the power of receptivity does not mean waiting for some Leader or Boss, or even inaction, but means participating naturally in change, allowing growth to happen — growth which can only be stifled or warped, but which can never be ego-determined or hurried.

For decades Meridel LeSueur has been telling her vision of the new emergence of power and creativity in women, and of the social import of this power; we are only beginning to understand what she means. So catch the lilt of the chant to the Grandmother; feel the long centuries of submerged power now breathing through you and wanting to call out its name. Don't be surprised to find your own lost name chiming in echo.

Mary Ellen Shaw

CONTENTS

Rites of Ancient Ripening

LET THE VOICE OF THE PEOPLE BE HEARD!

Midwest Villages & Voices
3451 Cedar Avenue South
Minneapolis, Minnesota 55407

This book is being re-issued by Meridel LeSueur with production and distribution assistance from Midwest Villages & Voices. We want to take this opportunity to share our vision with the Readers.

The villages and the cities of the Midwest resound with unheard voices.

Midwest Villages & Voices wants these voices to be heard, read and seen—in songs, poetry, interviews, prose, and the visual arts. Our efforts are just beginning and we want people to join us to make a vision bloom.

Midwest Villages & Voices believes that our language belongs to the people and shall return to us—the circle has a continuous and unending path.

We want to reclaim our literature, art and music and make it available to the public. There is a crying need for all of us to assist and promote writers and other artists who have a vision that encompasses the people of the world, that reveals truth and impressions in creative ways, that makes us feel the pulsing lifeblood of humanity.

Only a few select individuals have the resources to publish their own works. For the most part, publishing companies and editors remain remote from us and seem primarily concerned with what will sell the fastest and appeal to the largest number of people. There are a few exceptions in the publishing world, and we want to support their efforts and see more get a foothold.

Books and art must not be commodities to be produced, sold, and consumed. They are made from the creative efforts of people and are not financial investments to bring future profits to a few.

Midwest Villages & Voices maintains that groups like ours can promote, sell and review books and other projects in order to support and sustain artists and artisans. We think we can do it in a better way than do the large corporations that presently control what is available for us to read, write, hear, and discuss.

We need groups of people to establish themselves as part of Midwest Villages & Voices—to find books and projects, write books and poems and songs, read and edit books, photograph or find old photographs, raise money, keep lists of people, buy books before they are published to aid in getting them to the press, review books, distribute books, start reading groups, visualize with art, share skills of book production, make tapes to preserve oral history, and so on.

When someone writes a book or illustrates a vision, we want to discuss it, love it, help distribute it to others who will also want to read it and talk about it and share their feelings about it. We want to help writers and other artists in ways we can, whether that be aiding in editing, production or sales. We want people to make their skills available to others and join us in these efforts.

To listen to the people, to speak to the people—these are the springs from which our dreams flow!

MIDWEST VILLAGES & VOICES

Meridel Le Sueur, Rachel Tilsen, David Tilsen
John Crawford, Karen Northcott, Gayla Wadnizak Ellis

WINTERS OF THE SLAIN

HUSH, MY LITTLE GRANDMOTHER

Hush, my little grandmother
I am a woman come to speak for you.
I am a woman speaking for us all
From the tongue of dust and fire
From the bowl of bitter smoke.
This is a song for strength and power.
Water is pouring
                water is running,
The drouthy blooms,
It is coming out pouring in bloom of day.
Let us all go down there and bathe in the water.
The water is coming on the four paths of the eagles.
Let us all, of many colors, go down where the waters come
Calling   calling to us   in rivers of wind and blood.
We are floods
              We are Apache plumes
We are the brave cacti's rosy blossom,
Forgetting the thorns   and the dry
We are glut of a strong thrust grandmother.
Hush   hush, my little root
My empty pod,
Hush   hush, my little grandmother,
I am a woman come to speak
    in tongues of dust and fire,
Woman bowled
            and filled with pollen.

I LIGHT YOUR STREETS

I am a crazy woman with a painted face
On the streets of Gallup.
I invite men into my grave
                for a little wine.
I am a painted grave
Owl woman   hooting for callers in the night.
Black bats over the sun sing to me
The horned toad sleeps in my thighs,
My grandmothers gave me songs to heal
But the white man buys me cheap without song
      or word.
My dead children appear and I play with them.
Ridge of time in my grief — remembering
Who will claim the ruins?
           and the graves?
                the corn maiden violated
As the land?
I am a child in my eroded dust.
I remember feathers of the hummingbird
And the virgin corn laughing on the cob.
Maize defend me
Prairie wheel around me
I run beneath the guns
           and the greedy eye
And hurricanes of white faces knife me.
But like fox and smoke I gleam among the thrushes
And light your streets.

RUN RUN   COME COME

I am horizon that runs from your central breast
Curve you in embrace
Central where you left the skull and tree and the
                blood on sacrificial grass.
In my white buffalo robe
                I rise from all massacres.
I am the heat. I am your brave heart.
I am the scalp in your hand.
I am the severed arm speaking
           the amputated limbs
           the frozen mothers
The babes drinking at the frozen breasts.
I am rising from the bloody carnage
I am the ghost of Blunt Knife's Band going north
I am Black Hawk's song
I am a woman warm in the herbage of your embrace.
I was your child beside your thigh.
I am your sister beside you
             bone and sinew
              skin and skull
Running from the tide of gunshot.
Run run   come come
For my sake let us arrive together.
Dig me from the cougared dust
Where I lie waiting you in fire and thorn.
From my feet burst the prairie grasses.
Do not withhold your strength or your power.
Our beauty comes from the generosity of your loins
Fed by antelope and deer   let your blood bloom
             at the sight of maidens.
Run run   come come
The same enemy pursues us
              the same mother guards us
Run into my flowering prairie
            run   run.

DEAD IN BLOODY SNOW

I am an Indian woman
Witness to my earth
Witness for my people.
I am the nocturnal door,
The hidden cave of your sorrow,
Like you hidden deep in furrow
        and dung
    of the charnel mound,
I heard the craven passing of the
        white soldiers
And saw them shoot at Wounded Knee
        upon the sleeping village,
And ran with the guns at my back
Until we froze in our blood on the snow

I speak from old portages
Where they pursued and shot into the river crossing
All the grandmothers of Black Hawk.
I speak from the smoke of grief,
        from the broken stone,
And cry with the women crying from the marsh
Trail and tears of drouthed women,
      O bitter barren!
      O barren bitter!
I run, homeless,
      I arrive
   in the gun sight,
        beside the white square houses
   of abundance.
      My people starve
In the time of the bitter moon.
I hear my ghostly people crying
    A hey a hey a hey.

Rising from our dusty dead the sweet grass,
The skull marking the place of loss and flight.
I sing holding my severed head,
             to my dismembered child,
A people's dream that died in bloody snow.

LOST MOTHER LODE

I am hitchhiking with wolves
Ahead of the border snatchers.
Get a dark girl to change your luck,
Two bits is enough for an Indian.
Watch out for the white cop
Wherever you go they are upon you
    stretched over you
Throw you from a car when they are done,
The plantation boys standing around
Not a rainbow over you
Only darkness and greed and white faces.
I wander about
My village lost
Lost woman mine
Lost mother lode
Mine me.
Let the plantation boys hunger and thirst
Let the Fort soldiers die
Let the farmers cease plowing with alien plows.
Do not plow my flesh any more
Do not impregnate me without intention and love.
I wander about
                Beware of me
White slavers
I do not rattle before I strike.

BEHOLD ME! TOUCH ME!

Behold me
        crying to you brothers.
Hear my people crying on the trail of tears.
Return the buried children to me
Return the mutilated hands
           the cut off ears,
Return the tiny embryo
The prairie dark
        drouthed women,
The silent cricket
         the poisoned bird,
Behold me
        I am the daily bread
        I am the daily breast.
The eastern dawn striped egg
        cracks and breaks.
Behold us
Crying to you, brothers!
I come toward you shouting
To call you to the land of meeting, brothers.
Fat buffalo   stalwart people   and a holy tree
  of liberty flourishing for all birds
          for all children.
Contain me!
      Invite me!
         Behold me!
I come toward you shouting
Do not let them kill me before you speak to me
Touch me!
      Behold me!

NO ENEMY FACES

None of it was true about our enemies.
                              We have none.
Women never birth enemy faces
An enemy face is never born
No walls, barriers, closed wombs
The barren and the breastless summer
                              sings
To the face of lovers.

Birth is with others
                and given.

I HAVE COME TO WALK AMONG YOU

I have come to walk among the drouth when love is gone.
I have deep fathers
                sunk within my breast
Their bones are restless in the land
Their flesh turned by alien plows
Turning up dust of deep remembrance
I look down in the flooded rivers
                and see grief
  flooding the dust
                pressed down by
  the hooves of conquerors.
Floating, waiting for thunder the
              drowned faces of
  ripe sons and daughters.
You have had your flesh of us
Turned to your plow
              summer bright
  and upbloomed dust.
O conqueror, give up the stolen deed
Clear and fall ripe in
              your own harvest.
Be wild sumac, tasseled corn
              and love,
And I will warm your feet
              between my breasts.
I am field of long ago
              plowed and forgotten
And I come to walk among you
              planting abundant corn.

GREEN UNFURL ME

I have prepared a smoke for you
        husbands   fathers
          brothers   hunters.
Restore thou for me my bruised body,
Restore my bleeding feet to fruit.
Heal me of insult.
              Bear me from hell.
In the middle of the wide blue earth
I am crying   crying
Fragmented in ruins, my blind brother
Taught me to sing and prepare a smoke for you.
My blind sister taught me a song to sing
Blind over my harp   my plucked strings.
The knife cuts   I scream silence,
Blood of women makes the mulberry red.
The fruits of my valley juiced by the blood
              of massacres.
I have received it like earth within my flesh.
Rainbowed round in lighted ruins
I have walked into your gunsight,
And received your split bullet
In my upturned flesh.
My bowl filled with your filth,
I have borne you in drouth and glut.
I am prone   lying on the ground.
I am prone my dusty feet and hair
           caked in the spittled dust,
In the violated cave.
I lie prone   father husband,
Open me kernel, green unfurl me
Reach green to my hungry heart, husband.
Potent grain and crop await your breast
Reach green to my hungry breast
              into my dust of fire and thorn
And face me to your knife of love.

TOUCH MY COB

Down to the green tomb
Open the corn
Kernel the cob, brother
Open in green furl
          sugar and green.

Reach through the corn, brother,
Reach through the green to my heart
Reach, brother, male twin in the corn
Touch my cob
          and we will be together
              as bread.

CHANGING WOMAN

ALL AROUND ME, COME!

I am the female white shell
Come to me
Come come come come come.
All comes spike and calyx
All around me
        Come!
My grandmother said,
I took you out of your mother
I held you against my own thighs
       to warm you.
I gave you the mother cob
You are the Katchina girl.
And all is beautiful.
The flower head   the curving neck
  the meadowed breast
  the horizon belly   curve of buttock
  stretch of legs   the bottom of the feet
All beautiful, she said
       root earth and She Rain.
       As I lie on the earth
Be upon me
     Take me
       I am powerful!

SEPULCHRE IN BUD

Cocoons of children's faces
     bloom in spring
Struck child out of explosions of calcium
Out of bondage out of silence chaos
Torrents of flesh,
From sepulchre and bud
      the child comes,
From the human dried burnt enduring buried
He springs.
Cocoons of children's faces opening
     out of time rock bone
  and singing
      without armor or gun
        naked bud.
Bone flowers rock out of poisoned strontium
Out of the land of massacre genocide
We brought him
  escaping marked doors of murder.
Ancestors walked out of the wilderness in him
  unrolled the flesh
      flowered the bone
Sprang from rock
  lyre from bone
      enemies as flowers
Strike and swing rock-a-bye child
The bone will sing — rock.

SHELTER HIM IN MILK AND MEADOW

Out of the bitter herb   the splintered bone
You came child.
The nucleus arrived at gentle in him.
Cradle amidst satellites.
Orbit the tiny breast   the true ellipse of milk
Out of feudal darkness
              leaping into daffodils.
Into landscape out of ruin
Into pastures we never knew.
Hills of bluebells always ringing in
              the great wishes
   always arriving.
From mother clay the expansions of millions.
Brain and belly alight in spring solstice.
The common day turned marvelous.
And the hemisphere lighted by millions
              of children.
They will break the stone of bondage,
              of silence.
Summer squash and bean rejoice,
Pitch and cry of earth turns.
Approach of swarm, singing over horizons
              and peripheries.
Spreading body of one man or woman
              girdling the earth.
Sheltered bursting seed   make it safe
              for us forever.
The child perpetually appearing
              with us forever.
Shelter him in milk and meadow.
              Shelter.

BUDDED WITH CHILD

Before your cry
     I never heard a cry,
Headless ghost I rode the prairies,
The bodiless head screaming after me,
Skeleton, I searched for rose and flesh,
Lamenting in bereaved villages
Howling in stone cities.
I gave berries to strangers
I gave them fruits
          I gave them fruits
For stones and bones and broken words.
In the place where crying begins
The place of borders, the place of the enemy
I begot you, child,
Before you I did not know flowers
         out of snow,
Or milk of meadows out of drouth.
Before your cry I never heard a cry,
Or globular breast, milk without summons.
Exiled I cried along the rivers
         caged in time and loss,
Empty pod I longed for winged seeds.
Till merged in earth's agony of birth
        leapt bridge
        struck lyre
Impaled on earth and flesh's spring,
        budded with child.
Before you, child, I never knew the breast of milk
      the arm of love
        the kerneled grain of groats
   and all for bread.
Before your face I never saw a face descending
        down my belly to time's horizon
Breast and skin multiplied into multitude
      and benevolence.

SPRANG SEED TO WIND

Before you came
I never slept with hope
            or hoped for flesh.
Sprang seed to wind
            spiraled petal to light
Or leapt from root to calyx
            or sprang through time and space
                        Alive!
Child, you always bring the summer
   of earth and flesh
                        the summer comes,
For they say and I say
            that all bloom and flesh,
All passes through spike and ovary
Whistle and breath,
                        constant love
   multiplied
            naked
                        and forever

Perpetual Child!

BEHOLD THIS AND ALWAYS LOVE IT

O my daughters
My bowl is full of sweet grass,
I approach in my best buckskin,
I travel the path of the people
Behold me!
The white buffalo woman brings the
                    sacred pipe of vision.
Standing on the hill behold me
          Coming   coming   coming.
Over the prairie breast I come
                sacred,
Covered by a cloud of flowers.
Behold what you see, my grandchildren
                    Behold this
And always love it.

She moves   she moves   all moves to her.
In the bowl   the basket   the earth bowl
She is adorned in the middle country
She appears in the crops of Kansas.
In Oklahoma brothels,
In erupting volcanoes,
At the peyote ceremony of birds.
In the hell holes and the heavenly meadows
            she appears.
From far away she is coming   coming
From all the roads she is coming   coming.
They are gathering.   They are coming.
The ancients are coming with the children.
From far away they are coming   incessantly
                        coming.
Send out a crier, she says
                I want to talk to the people.
Listen   Listen   while you are walking
All is upon the earth and all is sacred.

OFFER ME REFUGE

My prairie people are my home
Bird I return flying to their breasts.
Waving out of all exiled space
They offer me refuge
To die and be resurrected in their
                seasonal flowering.
My food their breasts
              milked by wind
Into my starving city mouth.

RITES OF ANCIENT RIPENING

I am luminous with age
In my lap I hold the valley.
I see on the horizon what has been taken
What is gone   lies prone   fleshless.
In my breast I hold the middle valley
The corn kernels cry to me in the fields
                    Take us home.
Like corn I cry in the last sunset
Gleam like plums.
                    My bones shine in fever
Smoked with the fires of age.
Herbal, I contain the final juice,
Shadow, I crouch in the ash
                    never breaking to fire.
Winter iron bough
                    unseen my buds,
Hanging close I live in the beloved bone
Speaking in the marrow
                    alive in green memory.
The light was brighter then.
Now spiders creep at my eyes' edge.
I peek between my fingers
                        at my fathers' dust.
The old stones have been taken away
                    there is no path.
The fathering fields are gone.
The wind is stronger than it used to be.
My stone feet far below me grip the dust.
I run and crouch in corners with thin dogs.
I tie myself to the children like a kite.
I fall and burst beneath the sacred human tree.
Release my seed and let me fall.

Toward the shadow of the great earth
                              let me fall.
Without child or man
                         I turn   I fall.
Into shadows,
                    the dancers are gone.
My salted pelt stirs at the final warmth
Pound me death
                       stretch and tan me death
Hang me up, ancestral shield
                           against the dark.
Burn and bright and take me quick.
Pod and light me into dark.

Are those flies or bats or mother eagles?
I shrink   I cringe
Trees tilt upon me like young men.
The bowl I made I cannot lift.
All is running past me.
The earth tilts and turns over me.
I am shrinking
    and lean against the warm walls of old summers.
With knees and chin I grip the dark
Swim out the shores of night in old meadows.
Remember   buffalo hunts
Great hunters returning
Councils of the fathers to be fed
Round sacred fires.
The faces of profound deer who
                           gave themselves for food.
We faced the east the golden pollened
                        sacrifice of brothers.
The little seeds of my children
                        with faces of mothers and fathers
Fold in my flesh
                    in future summers.

My body a canoe turning to stone
Moves among the bursting flowers of memory
Through the meadows of flowers and food,
I float and wave to my grandchildren in the
Tepis of many fires
              In the winter of the many slain
I hear the moaning.
I ground my corn daily
In my pestle many children
Summer grasses in my daughters
Strength and fathers in my sons
All was ground in the bodies bowl
       corn died to bread
         woman to child
           deer to the hunters.
Sires of our people
Wombs of mothering night
Guardian mothers of the corn
Hill borne torrents of the plains
Sing all grinding songs
   of healing herbs
Many tasselled summers
         Flower in my old bones
        Now.
Ceremonials of water and fire
Lodge me in the deep earth
   grind my harvested seed.
The rites of ancient ripening
Make my flesh plume
And summer winds stir in my smoked bowl.
Do not look for me till I return
        rot of greater summers
Struck from fire and dark,
Mother struck to future child.

Unbud me now
Unfurl me now
Flesh and fire
   burn
    requicken
     Death.

SURROUND OF RAINBOWS

LET THE BIRD OF EARTH, FLY!

I send my voice of sorrow
      calling calling
My bowl is full of grief
         and the wind is up.
Thanks, all the people are crying
Behold and listen!
All is grown here
       where the sun goes down,
The world within our hands
       flies upward like a bird.
All that moves rejoices.
Approach each other as relatives
I give you corn
        I give you love
He he eyee eyee
Let the bird of the earth loose,
  dove from the dark ark.
Flood out of the horizoned breast
The human flesh lighted
        like a lamp.
All lighted
     corn beetle
       and hill of dust
Hey a hey
    and thanks   grandmother!

STRUCK FLESH DRUMMED

The rains will come
For we know the spirit of our ancestors
                    and honor them,
I heard the whistling women   in the wind,
All heard the women crying
                    from Tierra del Fuego
To the north pole,
                    and the drums spoke
    and the dogs bayed,
It is time to feed the angry spirits
                    it is time
To listen to the weeping of the wind women.
We saw them all night, spirits of our dead
Cheeks bulging with whistling air
Brine on the cheeks
                    rattle of bones
Struck flesh drummed.
The men fell softly, ancestral mothers over them,
The gourds trembled
                    the seeds shook,   burst,
The whistling women   thrummed   roused in Blue Thunder

And the rains came.

COME TO MY SINGING, WE ARE HOME

We will make a home amongst the robbers.
In the piñon boughs
On the blackblue, yellow and white wind,
I travel upon you free.
Mix the dust of ancestors with manure and
    give us home.
The animals come to our singing
To our turquoise home of the sky
Our fathers' house.
Make a fire brothers they cannot take the fire.
A circle of stone will be sacred.
We have purified the water of deliverance.
It is clear and sacred.
Under your curtain of He Rain
                    I shall sleep.
No evil shall come to pass with your dark horn
                    over me.
Under your prairie breast streaming in the
                    four directions
Under your dark hair
                    let us sleep.
All is given in the place of emergence.
In the house of death where I had no home
We shall be home
Eating with the mouth that had no food.
Alive in the breast they tried to empty.
In the six directions we take strength
We are home.

SURROUND OF RAINBOWS

The doorway to my home is made of light
Restore and return the body
                              call it home.
Walk toward me now
Let all tongues ring
Quicken the thighs and breast
                    the brain clangs
Strikes the horizon bell
                              all quickens
All things open in the She Rain.
Growing happily
              We return to our herds
                    to our hogans
                        to jingling tassels
                            belling of sheep.
Someone is drumming
                    beating the sky.
Corn reaches up
                    She Rain reaches down
Juices spring out of dry thorns
Forgotten bones flesh with forgotten men.
I entered the living water
                    It fell upon my starving bones.
Blue corn tied with white lightning
                    and the rains come
      upon me too.
Restore us all
The land the man the woman child beast
Insect   all creatures beasts and herbs
Restore us here
Tie us with the blue bean, the great squash
Surround of rainbows
                    Listen
The rain comes upon us
                    Restore us.

I HEAR YOU SINGING IN THE BARLEY RIPE

Put on your best buckskin
Approach in a beautiful manner
And sing!
O my children! O my children!
Look thus I shouted
                    when I moved the earth
                         when I moved the earth!
I hear you singing, child, in the barley ripe
                    Rich you grow
                    Earth's cradle swinging
The pitch of summer in all your flesh.
When I saw you approaching, my children, my children,
I then saw the multitude plainly
                         I saw them plainly approaching
And all the myriads, leap the bridge
And pass over
                    the perpetual and earthly child
Going to the endless fruit
                    Saved by us all!
Beautiful child, appearing in constellations
In all differences and repetitions
Future ancestors in a rain of seed.
Child   mother   grandmother   child again
I am singing it   I am singing it.
Look my children the earth is about to move.
I am humming to you   I am singing to you
I circle round and round the earth.
My father the whirlwind   we are running toward you
You are running toward us.
My children   My children   Here it is   I hand it to you
                    the earth!
                         the earth!
Put on your best buckskin
                    Pass over!

BRING US FORTH

O land of mother and father
                  Bring us forth!
Out of the seed sling
                        cradle green
                                    Bring us forth!
Turbulent prairie flower opened
                       and we sprang to light.
Space struck us out
                    broke us into speech.
Bell swung belled
                    flower out of stone,
Water from the rod
                    buds on the iron bough!

SMILING BEAST AND BREAD

Where are you going
      my children?
We are going to the fruit
      the fiber
         the seed
Of pollen ancestors.
It is the final road
And all is safe with us forever.
Child, where are you going?
I hear you singing, child, in the ripeness
   with smiling bread and beasts
      and mouths of flowers.
In the earth swung cradle
     in the gourd of honey
Rich you gloom
      round pit of dark,
In pitch of summer juiced and round.
Harbored by us all, child
     perpetual and earthly
   going to the endless fruit.
All tiny heads born constantly
      multiplied and safe
   with us forever.
Give us the child to pass over
     the golden pollen bridge,
Pass over to fiber and seed
     pass over.
Throw the spindle, leap the whole arch,
Pastures for colts, and a breast for all.
Future ancestors in a rain of children,
A jet of lovefire in swift runners,
Weave over   in the loom   throw the spindle
Throw my flowers when
      I'll never be gone.

CORN FOR ALL VILLAGES

We pray for all
The round earth is in the dance.
We will have watermelons,
The wild animals will be numerous.
We will have plenty of parched corn
        in all the villages of the world.
Hear these things at the dance.
The best things are being said.
We remember all the good things from our fathers,
The good flesh   the good heart   the good thought.
The corn is speaking from the field
As the harvesters eat:
See how lovingly man takes me home.
The mother will stoop and lift me saying:
I looked everywhere for you, little corn kernel
Where were you? Now you must come into my warm
        hand   my bosom.
Welcome, the house is open for all red, white, blue
Corn. We will rest. We are glad.
And the harvesters say: See the good corn
It wants to be harvested now See how it shakes.
We will not hurt you. The tassels tremble the
   cob shakes like a rattle of green.
Do not miss any kernels or you will hear them crying
Come on   let us harvest the corn!

RAISE THE FRUIT

In the winter solstice
       the returning sun
Brings the enormous and perpetual
          harvest.
In hunger and darkness
We drink the communal light,
Rising with all creatures
       into the perpetual
         rising sun.
Rising in ancestral dust
       from furrow of dung and blood.
Out of absence
Rising in pollen
    we await each other.
Earth roused will bring us home
        in seed and pollen.
Dance the ceremonial together
        in the entire solar light.
Sun shining on all friends.
O meet me in the unbombed villages
         of the earth.
In cobs of corn
In the dust   flesh
In the resurrected wheat
Forgive the root
       and raise the fruit!

MAKE THE EARTH BRIGHT   AND THANKS

I am making the sacred smoke
That all the people may behold it.
We are passing with great power
            over the prairie.
The light is upon our people
Making the earth bright
Feathers of sage and cedar
          upon our breasts
Shaking on wrists, ankles,
The tail of the red fox lighting us.
We are crying for a vision.
Behold me that my people may live.
Our people are generous
This is our day.
Your ancestors have all arrived.
The past has arrived
            Behold!
             Listen!

All is established here
We are relatives.
This planet earth
           and all upon it
Turns into view.
This earth is in our hands
Let it fly, bird of earth and light
All that moves will rejoice
Hey a hey a hey!
Approach in a beautiful manner
Approach in your best buckskin
Thanks, all the people are crying
And thanks, grandmother of the center
Of the earth
         Thanks!

STRIKE US TO BUD

Summer surrounds.
Strike us in fire and bud,
Bird   fly over the low horizon
                of my breast
Over the holocaust of burning cities
    fly over, bird.
                Do not fear the bomb, birds,
that falls and generates death.
I fly with you to Antibes, to Atlantis
And see far below the faces of my fathers,
    upthrust in death.
Comingle with the fires of space
    where we are buried and birthed.
My father tips this space to flint and fire.
My mother wombs this space in moisture and love.
Struck vein and flower in me
Down the fiery vein to vortex and whirl
Prophecy and pattern of seed love
Illumine my summer dark.
Napalmed children come to bud in woman dark.
Pour down container of cyclones
Quick flash of flesh and memory, bird.
Fly in the green of my flesh
In the green of my sleep flash, bird,
Touch and rouse in summer surrounds
Not rockets, but birds, fly over
                cover me
And I shake my rattles   drum them down
We shall reach harvest
                We shall make cob.
Tassel and shake and summer me here.

DÒAN KÊT

The Village has always lain in the path of the conqueror.
The villages of Viet Nam, of Africa, of Peru and Brazil, of Ireland,
Spain, Mexico, Cuba, Haiti, Iowa, New Mexico, Thailand, look up in
anger at the sky filled with fire, at napalm burning crops and skin,
and still they plunder the Village and the Villagers.

The Puritans plundered villages from coast to coast; drove the Cherokees
on the Trail of Tears, threw smallpox infected clothes into the Mandan
villages, Kit Carson drove the Navajos off their lands into the concentration
camps; north of Trinidad, Colorado, you can see the monument over
the Black Hole of Ludlow, a tent village burned by Rockefeller. Cortez
marched over the bodies of the Indian villages, destroyed from Ohio to
Tierra del Fuego; Hearst left a village of skulls at the mines of Potosí.
My family fled the Irish villages taken over for sheep runs for the mills of
Newcastle. My Iowa village is owned by absentee landlords now. Name
Lidice, the villages of pogroms, Guernica; from the Big Horn to Viet Nam —
the Massacre of Wounded Knee to the Mekong Delta, the same Village —
our Village.

COMMUNAL GLOBAL DAY

Let us seek each other in the villages of the earth,
In the root dark where we live in the dust,
Find us singing in the underground vein, the germinal seed,
    in the returning sun,
And bring our goodness to enormous, fertile and perpetual harvest,
    toward zeniths of noon.
Toward total expansions in crops of brotherhood and sisterhood.

Let us await each other in the village field,
In the new year, risen in ancestral dust, from the furrow,
From the loom of the people where, amid lamentations
We have loomed our life in pollen;
Where the leaves forgive the root
    and our children rise in perpetual sunrise, in immense globular light.
We await each other!

The light returns on no enemy faces,
    but upon the communal chorus,
Roused in villages of the earth, to cry salute and sing,
Shout in choruses of millions,
Rising toward communications, toward extremities of nadirs
Of total expansions, in the entire solar light, on all flesh,
On all fields and all villages
Roused from sleep, rouse us,
Let us seek each other and move from the violent, the broken, the predatory,
    to the enormous and myriad fertile and impregnated harvest,
    the global village
We sing with you in choruses of millions.

CORRIDOS OF LOVE

I am ahunger for my dark sisters, for my dark burning brothers.
Have you appetite for us the white kin of various hue,
ruddy farmers, mothers, fathers of milk and honey and work?
We hunger, hemisphere for hemisphere, to rondure,
Root and bud, pollen falling, humus in the dark.
We come to kiss where the borders disappear and all alien
faces drown in a river of tears and blood,
full of the perishing labor of millions.
I hear you crying below the borders
Grandfathers and Grandmothers of Indo-America,
the dust full of your ancient flesh —
the earth a dark woman lamp — burning.
To hear you
        to touch you
                to embrace you at last
Turned in the sun from the Bering Strait to Tierra del Fuego
the cup of clay, imperial chalice of man, woman, bird, beast!
Rounding in the brown and white, yellow and red hands,
turned to globular light, hung green in darkness;
Awaiting each other we flew in the wind of all pollen
on golden days, searching,
from antarctic to tropical light — from storms arising north
In the earth named Americas.
I say it now and hunt you out —
warriors of our dark nuptial male corn
and Cambian Indian mothers of the dark —
the Americas my love.
Tell me — the brown woman below the border asked me —
Can you reverse the verdict of darkness?
Tell me, my sister — she said — burning below you
crying below you is the
volcanic fire —

crying of crones, whores, mothers, saints, trampled by the boots of conquerors
doomed in infant flesh!
Stolen the hourly grief
                    Stolen the flesh and the time
                              Stolen the milk and the man.
Didn't you hear the hurricane of bare feet?
                    In the bloody span of dust there was my multiple face
                              there was my river of grief
                                        there was my enraged womb.
Didn't you hear me crying?
In Morelos, home of Zapata, thirty-two people owned the entire nation.
— a single woman owned twelve million of my acres.
Seventy percent of the babies used to die — a hill of skulls marked the mines of Potosí.
One quarter of the males died in three months.
Four out of five died in the silver mines.
The life of the plantation worker was seven years.
Doesn't the north hear the whip of lash, cry of peonage, bondage, starvation
as we are consumed by the conqueror?
Who stole two thirds of our nation?
Who buried the young Yankees at Vera Cruz and Chapultepec?
                    Were they your grandfathers?
Didn't you hear me plowing with my fingernails?
Or the sound of the spades of a million small graves?
Did our pain rise above the border you stole?
Was your sky darkened with our darkness?
Do you pay duty at the border of pain?
Have you a visa to permit you to feel it?
And I said to her:
I saw your Aztec face in a flock of birds flying over my farm.
I looked down with you at all the Americas,
at the great and common robbers — U.S. Steel, fruit companies,
Standard Oil, Hearst who stole my land, too,   Rockefeller, Mellon, Hill,
and the nameless now, the anonymous assassin, faceless, the cartel —
weasel continually consuming us, robbers, eroders, nocturnal assassin at
the vein — diseases   wounds   excavations.
Who has stolen the pump handle key to water, boarded up the source?

The old plow grieves lost to your hand, grandfathers.
Massacres of flesh and land, signatures of greed, lie on my land as well.
My women in Kansas, dried, rootless — screams of erosion and birth in
the dry wind. Tumbleweed women blowing in dust and eaten by the myriad
mandibles of grasshoppers.
Tiny seeds with children's faces move in a hurricane of grief
through the tunnel of midwest tornadoes of wind,
Thunderbolts of crashing air. Grip my hand as the hurricane passes.
Indians fill the air — pilgrims cry as they pass
the flint of our silence sparks to cry
in the acidic and bitter stone. I found the message, the agony of the
nocturnal assassin.
It is I — I have received his knife and taken him to bed!
We have wakened screaming at the same savage face of the predator,
     above us!
My village has disappeared in ruin and deadly wind!
I have tasted the calcium radiation of the dust,
and hear the announcement — keep your children in, today's snow is
radioactive! Sulphuric fright now appears in wheat and corn and
in the bread and salt the mutations of future idiots.

I seek and find you in the root dark,
In the underground veins the skeletal support of all leaves and
summer forgiven,
Germinal seed and seminal child of
Morelos and Chiapas — Ohio and Kansas
Navajos and Hopis — Irish and Dutch.
Quietly between us we have made the corn from windy grass,
to solid and bursting sun upon a stable cob.
Amidst lamentations, wounds, separations and lesions,
continuously and massively bruised under the hooves of conquerors.
we have loomed our lives,
with the same passion as high corn,
for the velocity of pollen spreading to all days.
As an ally I take you to my village.
In the diurnal green

the leaves forgive the root and raise the fruit!
I'm seeking you among the ancient stone!
In the dusty faces,
In the raised fist,
In the resurrected heart!

DÒAN KÊT

I

How can we touch each other, my sisters?
How can we hear each other over the criminal space?
How can we touch each other over the agony of bloody roses?
I always feel you near, your sorrow like a wind in the
great legend of your resistance, your strong and delicate strength.

It was the bumble bee and the butterfly who survived, not the dinosaur.

None of my sons or grandsons took up guns against you.

And all the time the predators were poisoning the humus, polluting
the water, the hooves of empire passing over us all. White
hunters were aiming down the gunsights; villages wrecked
mine and yours. Defoliated trees, gnawed earth, blasted embryos.

We also live in a captive country, in the belly of the shark.
The horrible faces of our predators, gloating, leering,
the bloody Ford and Rockefeller and Kissinger presiding over
the violation of Asia.

Mortgaging, blasting, claiming earth and women in the chorale
of flayed flesh and hunger, the air crying of carbon and thievery.

Our mutual flesh lights the sulphur emanation of centuries of
exploitation. Amidst the ruins we shine forth in holy mutual
cry, revealing the plainest cruelties and human equation,
the deprivations of power and the strength of numbers and
endurance and the holy light from the immortal wound.

---

*Dòan Kêt means "solidarity" in Vietnamese. This poem was sent to the
North Vietnamese Women's Union, where it was translated into Vietnamese
and warmly received. The poet received a letter of thanks from the women.

The only knowledge now is the knowledge of the dispossessed.
Our earth itself screams like a bandaged, roaring giant about
to rise in all its wounds and bear upon the conqueror.

Lock your doors in the cities.

There are no quiet dead — and no quiet deed.
Everything you touch now is ticking to its explosion.
The scab is about to infect.
The ruined land is dynamite. Cadmus teeth of dead guerrillas
gnaw the air. Nature returns all wounds as warriors.
The Earth plans resistance and cries, "Live".

What strikes you, my sisters, strikes us all. The global earth
is resonant, communicative.
Conception is instant solidarity of the child.
Simultaniety of the root drives the green sap of the flower.
In the broken, the dispossessed is the holy cry.

We keep our tenderness alive and the nourishment of the earth green.
The heart is central as lava.
We burn in each other. We burn and burn.
        We shout in choruses of millions.
        We appear armed as mothers, grandmothers, sisters, warriors.
        We burn.

II

Sisters, the predators plan to live within our bodies.
They plan to wring out of us unpaid labor.
Wrench their wealth from our bodies.
Like the earth they intend to bore inside the woman host,
open the artery like weasels, use, consume, devour, drill for
oil, eat the flesh of the earth mother.
Like the earth they will consume all woman flesh and the
commodities of her being.
The harbors of the world will be for the sale of her body.

The sweat shops will multiply stolen wealth of her living skin.
They slaver at the cheap labor of women around the world.
They will ground us on the metate, like living corn.
We will be gutted and used by the Companies to make wealth.
General Motors, Ma Bell, Anaconda, pickers of cotton and
coffee, hanging our babies on our backs, producers of hand
and brain and womb.
The world eaters sharpen their teeth.
Out of the unpaid labor of women they will triple their wealth.
Women far down under are trashed, pressed into darkness,
humiliated, exploited.
Half the women of Puerto Rico sterilized, the salt savor of
our sweat tiding like an ocean.
Brothels called meat markets in all the ports of the conqueror.

We are the wine cast struck to the ground, spilled.
We are a great granary of seed smashed, burned.
We are a garroted flight of doves.
We are face out of bone. Years of labor bend the bone and back.
Down the root of conquest our bodies receive the insult.
Receive a thousand blows, thefts of ovum and child.
Meadows of dead and ruined women. There is no slight death.
After the first death there is no other.
The Body trashed, dies.
There is no abstract death or death at a distance.
Our bodies extend into the body of all.
Every moment is significant in our solidarity.

In solidarity I stood at the gates of Honeywell where the "Mother
Bomb" is timed and triggered. I hid my grandsons from the gun.
I crouched under the terrible planes of Johnson, Nixon and
Kissinger.
I felt the boots on your throat as my own.
I saw the guns pointed at us all.
It was the gun used on my sister.

Now in the "white house" another mask of white criminals
turn upon us, on our native people at Wounded Knee, cut food for
our children and promise us a bigger army. Children are shot
down, I hear mothers crying from the black belt.

Women of the earth, bear the weight of the oppressor,
bearing us down into deep to glow upward from the dark,
from the womb, from the abyss of blood, from the injured
scream, from below we glow and rise singing.

III

I saw the women of the earth rising on horizons of nitrogen.
I saw the women of the earth coming toward each other
                        with praise and heat
                            without reservations of space.
All shining and alight in solidarity.
Transforming the wound into bread and children.
In a new abundance, a global summer.
Tall and crying out in song we arise
                            in mass meadows.
We will run to the living hills with our seed.
We will redeem all hostages.
We will light the bowl of life.
            We will light singing
                    across all seas
The resonance of the song of woman,
            lifted green, alive
            in the solidarity of the communal love.
Uncovering the illumined fruit
            the flying pollen
            in the thighs of golden bees
We bring to you our fire
            We pledge to you our guerilla
fight against the predators of our country.
We come with thunder
            Lightning on our skin,

Roaring womb singing
                  Our sisters
                          Singing.
Choruses of millions
                  Singing.

BIBLIOGRAPHY
Drawn in part from that compiled by Mary Kay Smith in CORN VILLAGE (Statton Lee, 1970), with additions by Mary Ellen Shaw, updated 1983.

BOOKS
ANNUNCIATION. Los Angeles, Platen Press, 1935
SALUTE TO SPRING. New York, International, 1940
NORTH STAR COUNTRY. New York, Duell, Sloan & Pearce, 1945 (American Folkways Series)
LITTLE BROTHER OF THE WILDERNESS. New York, Knopf, 1947
NANCY HANKS OF THE WILDERNESS ROAD. New York, Knopf, 1949 (Borzoi Books)
SPARROW HAWK. New York, Knopf, 1950 (Borzoi Books)
CHANTICLEER OF WILDNERNESS ROAD. New York, Knopf, 1951 (Borzoi Books)
THE RIVER ROAD. New York, Knopf, 1954 (Borzoi Books)
CRUSADERS. New York, Blue Heron Press, 1955
CORN VILLAGE, Sauk City, WI, Statton Lee, 1970
CONQUISTADORES. New York, Franklin Watts, 1973
MOUND BUILDERS. New York, Franklin Watts, 1974
HARVEST & SONG FOR MY TIME. 1929-1945.[4] West End, 1979
RIPENING. Feminist Press, 1982
THE GIRL. 1939.[4] West End, 1980
WORKER WRITERS. Handbook, 1939[4]. West End, 1982
NORTH STAR COUNTRY. People's History, 1945.[4] International Pubs., 1983

SELECTED STORIES, ARTICLES, POEMS
Nests (poem). POETRY, 24 (May 1924), 80-81
Persephone (story). DIAL, 82 (May 1927), 371-80[1]
Laundress (story). AMERICAN MERCURY, 12 (Sept. 1927), 98-101
The Afternoon (story). DIAL, 84 (May 1928), 386-98
Holiday (story). PAGANY, 1 (Spring 1930), 87-99
Spring Story (story). Reprinted from SCRIBNER'S MAGAZINE in O'BRIEN, BEST SHORT STORIES OF THE YEAR, 1931
Corn Village (story). SCRIBNER'S MAGAZINE, 90 (Aug. 1931) 133-40[2]
What Happens in a Strike (article). AMERICAN MERCURY, 33 (Nov. 1934), 329-35
Biography of My Daugher (story). AMERICAN MERCURY, 34- (Jan. 1935), 63-68[2]
A Hungry Intellectual (story). AMERICAN MERCURY, 34 (Feb. 1935), 154-59[2]
The Fetish of Being Outside (article). NEW MASSES (Feb. 26, 1935), 22-23
The Horse (story). STORY MAGAZINE (1935). Second prize in Federal Writers' Contest
The Bird (story). NEW CARAVAN, 1936
Tradesman La Salle (story). MANUSCRIPT (1936)
Annunciation (story). O'BRIEN, BEST SHORT STORIES OF THE YEAR, 1936[2]
The Girl (story). YALE REVIEW, 26 (Dec. 1936), 369-81[1,2]
God Make Little Apples (story). PRAIRIE SCHOONER (1937)
Gone Home (story). KENYON REVIEW, 7 (Spring 1945), 235-45
Breathe Upon These Slain (story). KENYON REVIEW, 7 (Summer 1945), 399-418[3]
O Prairie Girl Be Lonely (story). NEW CARAVAN (1945)
A Legend of Wilderness Road (story). CALIFORNIA QUARTERLY, 3 (Winter 1954), 3-9
Spring Came on Forever (story). PLAINSONG, 1 (Spring 1967) 5-19
Shelter Him in Milk and Meadow (poem). PRAIRIE SCHOONER, 44 (Winter 1969-70), 369

Other collections in which the author's work has appeared:
BEST ESSAYS OF 1936
PREFERENCES, 1936
THE NEW CARAVAN, 1938
CALIFORNIA STORY ANTHOLOGY, 1960

[1] Reprinted in O'BRIEN, BEST SHORT STORIES OF 1927 (Persephone) and 1938 (The Girl)
[2] Reprinted in SALUTE TO SPRING
[3] Reprinted in O'HENRY PRIZE STORIES OF 1946
[4] Date of writing if published much later

Rites of Ancient Ripening has been a beloved book. The first three printings were published by Vanilla Press. We have tried to preserve the loving creative work of Jean Marie Fischer and Vanilla Press in the original layout, typesetting, and design of this book.

This edition is published by Meridel Le Sueur and David Tilsen,
                additional typesetting by duck type,
                printed by Haymarket Press,
                with assistance from Midwest Villages and Voices.